UNDER THE SEA

UNDER THE SEA

Weird & Wonderful Creatures from the Deep

Photographs by
Youji Ohkata

Text by
Leighton Taylor

CHRONICLE BOOKS

SAN FRANCISCO

First published in the United States in 1993 by Chronicle Books.

Text copyright © 1993 by Chronicle Books. Photographs copyright © 1991 by Sankai-do Book Publishing Co., Ltd. All rights reserved. No part of this book may be reproduced in any form without written permission from Chronicle Books.

Printed in Japan.

Library of Congress Cataloging-in-Publication Data

Ohkata, Youji, 1942-
  [Marin burū. English]
  Under the sea : weird & wonderful creatures from the deep
photographs by Youji Ohkata ; text by Leighton Taylor.
      p. cm.
    ISBN 0-8118-0263-9 (paperback)
  1. Marine fauna—Pictorial works. 2. Deep-sea fauna—Pictorial
  works.   I. Taylor, L.R. (Leighton R.) II. Title.
    QL121.03513 1993
      591.92—dc20   92-40517
                          CIP

Cover & text design: Alison Berry

Cover photograph: Youji Ohkata

Distributed in Canada by
Raincoast Books
112 East Third Avenue
Vancouver, B.C. V5T 1C8

10 9 8 7 6 5 4 3 2 1

Chronicle Books
275 Fifth Street
San Francisco, California 94103

CONTENTS

Feather star and pink sea fan

INTRODUCTION

Even a snorkeler's shallow view of a living coral reef supports one's faith that the life of the oceans has become progressively richer and more beautiful since the earth began billions of years ago. Although such a progression of richness may not have been steady—life happens in fits and starts—a vital impetus toward complexity is certain. Youji Ohkata's extraordinary photographs give us a glimpse of the richness of the coral reefs spread throughout the tropical Pacific and Indian oceans. Each photograph has its own splendor and aesthetic appeal, and each also reveals and exemplifies some great biological phenomenon of coral reefs. There is more to each picture than initially meets the eye. Perhaps a quick review of basic marine biology will be helpful in enjoying and understanding these images.

All living things are faced with the same three challenges: to eat (most plants, of course, do not actively "eat"; they manufacture food through photosynthesis using energy from sunlight to process water and carbon dioxide, assisted by nutrients from the soil or other

sources), to avoid being eaten, and (most important to the species) to reproduce. The mechanisms (called "adaptations" by biologists) by which plants and animals strive to achieve these goals are wondrously diverse, especially in the tropical habitats of coral reefs.

It is difficult to categorize each adaptation, but it helps to consider them within an arbitrary framework of concepts. Quite a few are illustrated in the photographs, and include the following:

Calcification, or "structure-building," is the ability of many marine plants and animals to remove dissolved limestone chemicals from seawater and form them into hard skeletons. The most obvious examples of calcification are the stony branches of reef corals (see page 86). The white sands of tropical beaches and lagoon floors (see pages 62, 63) consist only of the calcified fragments of such animals and plants.

Territoriality is a complex behavior of animals, including fighting and cooperation focused on the sharing of resources on the reef (see pages 28, 73).

Sexual strategies, courting, breeding, and protection of young (see pages 12, 27), and even the change of an individual's gender during its lifetime, are part of the great panorama of sex on the reef.

Symbiosis, the close association of one organism with another resulting in some benefit for at least one of the two organisms (see pages 44, 61, 71, 87), gives rise to some of the most interesting phenomena on the reef.

Guilds are the various "ways of making a living" that reef animals use to survive. Examples among fishes include plankton-picking, ambushing, chasing, browsing, and cleaning (see pages 64, 71, 75).

Many of the species illustrated in this book are found throughout the Indo-Pacific area, and from the Red Sea to Mexico. There can be distinct regional differences, however. A few species are restricted to specific areas; on page 14, for example, is a fish known only from the Maldive Islands in the Indian Ocean. There are two main reasons for this widespread distribution of marine animals—the dynamic current patterns of the oceans and the planktonic, free-floating young of most reef species, even those that are as adults attached to the bottom. The great majority of marine organisms have double life-styles: young, wide-ranging, planktonic (driven by the currents) larval form and a later, sedentary life adult form. When one looks at the adult animals on a reef, one sees the children of marine animals that spawned perhaps hundreds of miles away, and one sees the parents of young that have settled far from their birth.

The best tools for getting the most from this book are your own careful eyes and an open mind. Like any artist, Youji Ohkata has included far more visual information, views, and perspectives than he intended, or perhaps is even aware of. Look carefully, enhance your own view, understanding and appreciation and keep in mind that much of what we see beneath the sea is so complex we do not yet understand it.

Feather star and scarlet sea fan

Blue-lined snapper

Banded jack

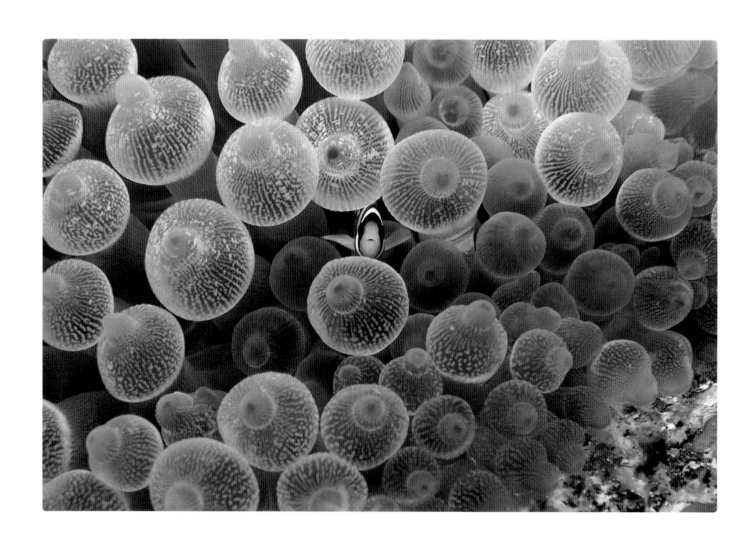

Juvenile anemonefish and anemone

Clown anemonefish and anemone

Maldive anemonefish and carpet anemone

Carpet anemone

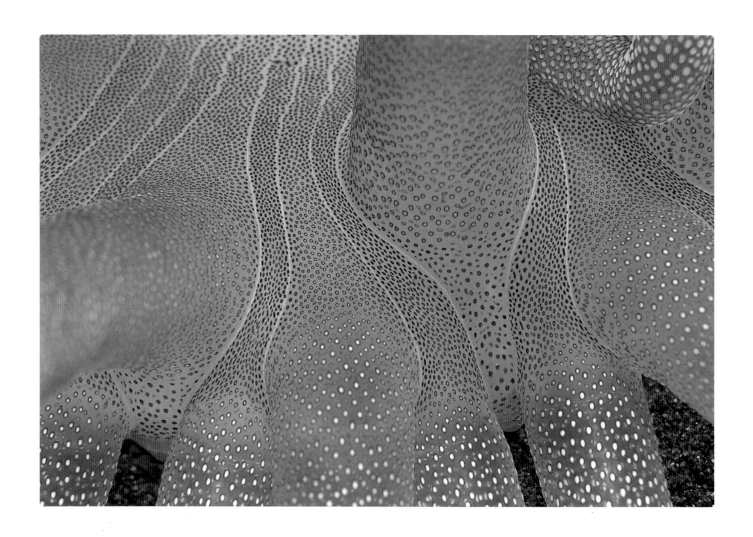

Armed sea anemone

Armed sea anemone

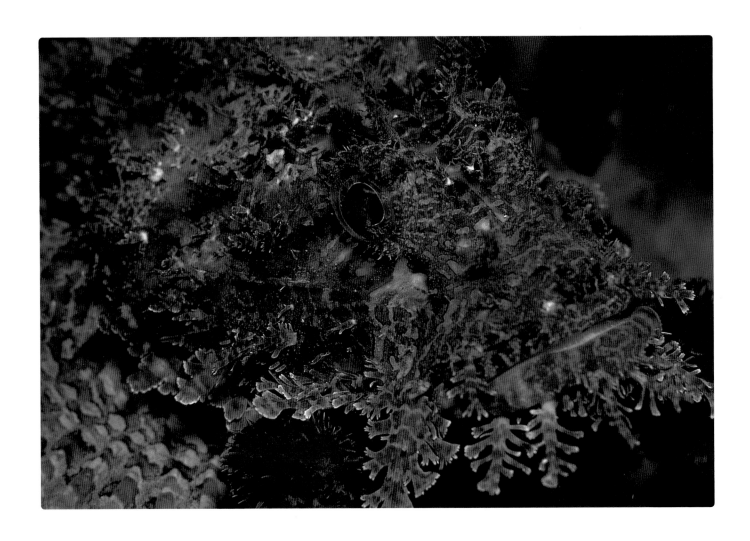

Raggy scorpionfish

Box crab

Juvenile needlefish

Chevron barracuda

Rockcod, wire coral and sponge

Hermit crab and fire coral

Slender cardinalfish and scarlet sea fan

Burrowing anemone

Black-tipped rockcod and octocoral

Moon wrasse and feather star

Yaeyama blenny *(left)* and neon triplefin *(right)*

Weber's chromis

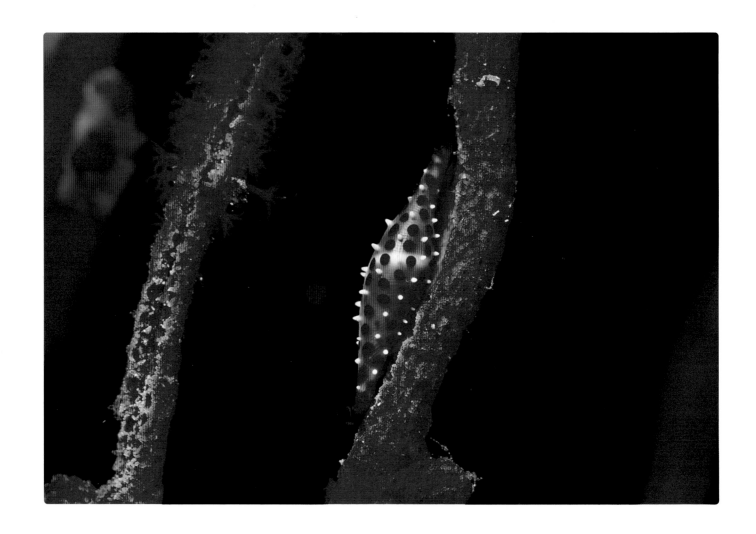

Spindle cowrie and red sea fan

Egg cowrie, soft coral and hard coral

Anemone shrimp and bubble coral

Bigmouth triplefin and white fire coral

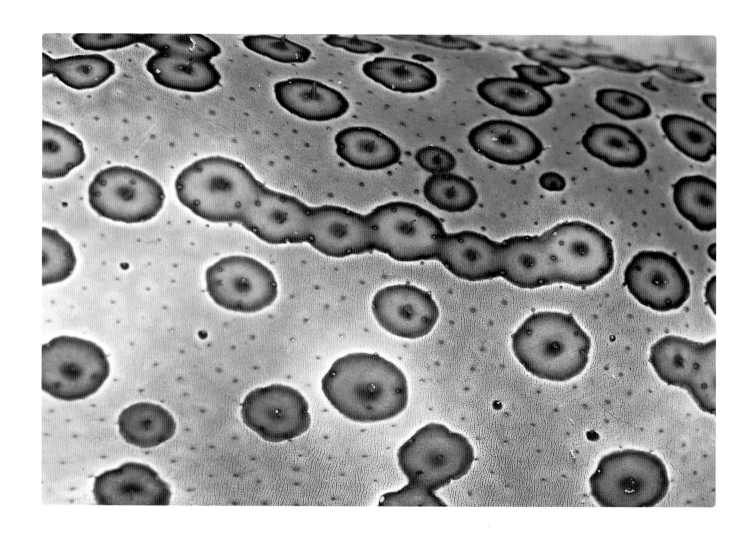

Bronze-spot sea cucumber

34

Pincushion starfish

Coral cod and cleaner wrasse

Coral cod and cleaner shrimp

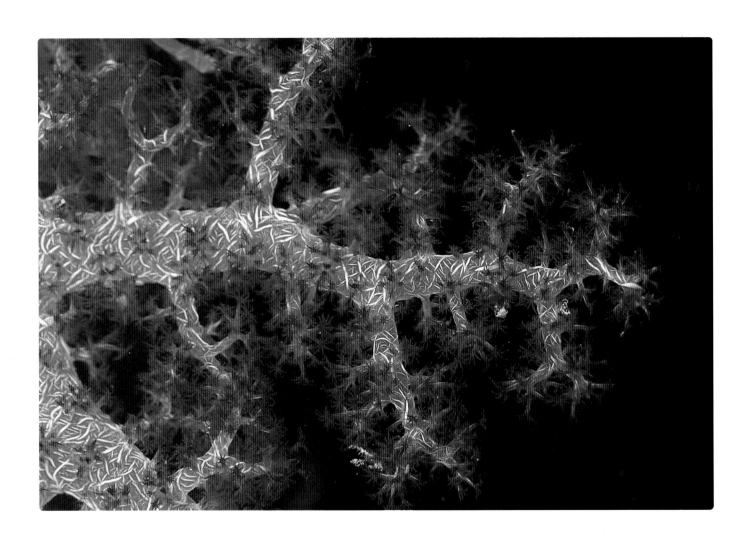

Soft coral

Two-lobed goby and soft coral

Coral goby and coral

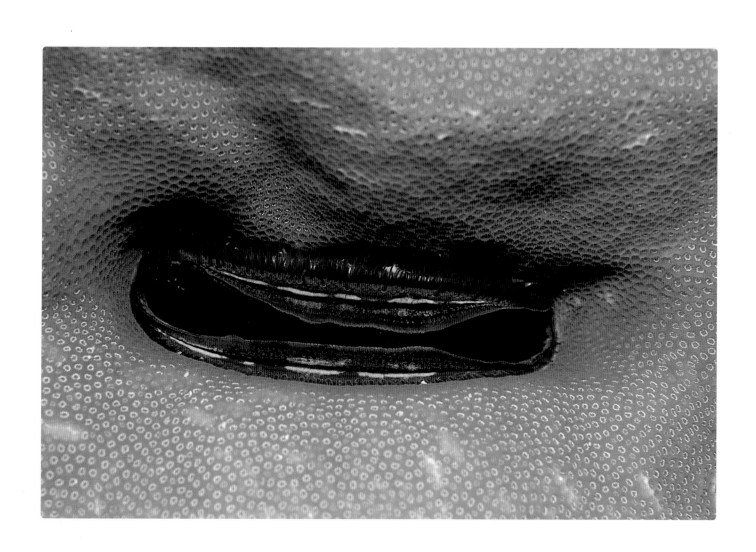

Red-eyed rock scallop and coral

Black-tipped rockcod

Dwarf hawkfish

Thornback cowfish

Gold hawkfish

Manta ray and slender suckerfish

Warty jellyfish

Purple dottyback

Threadfin dartfish

Freckled porcupinefish

Ragged-fin firefish

Coral

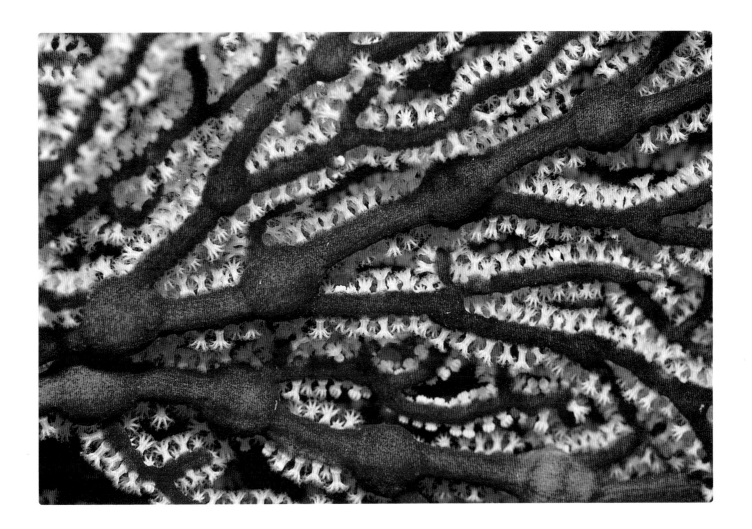

Scarlet sea fan

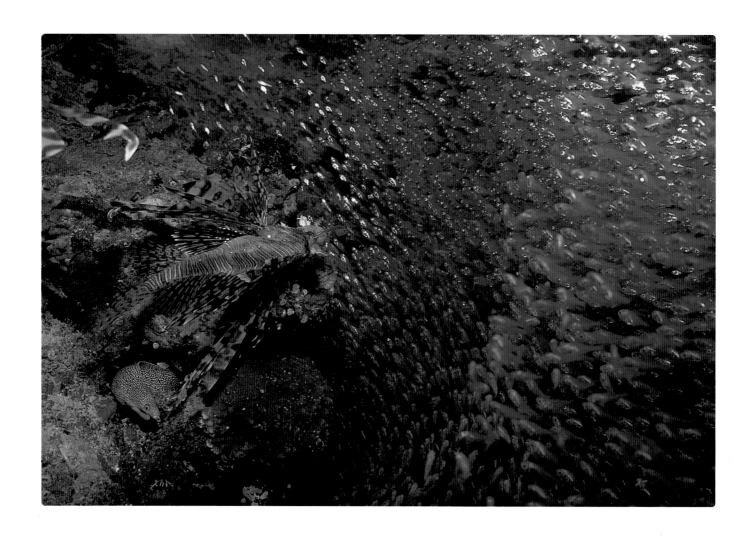

Moray eel and lionfish

Lionfish and golden sweeper

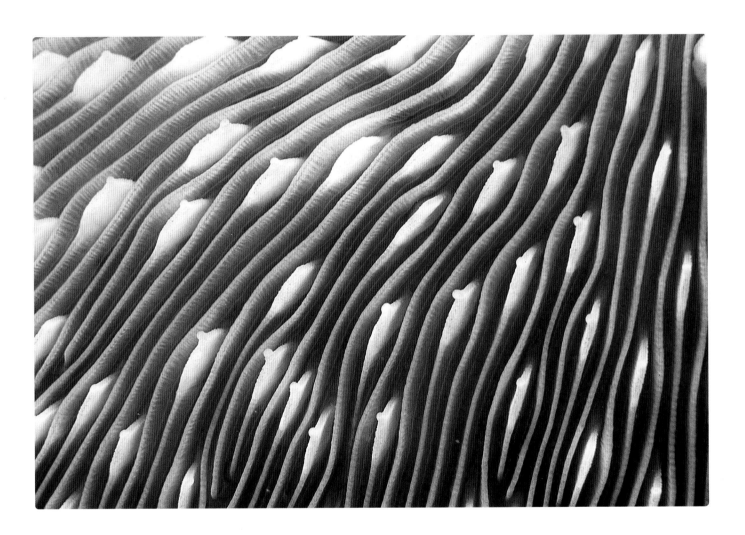

Mushroom coral

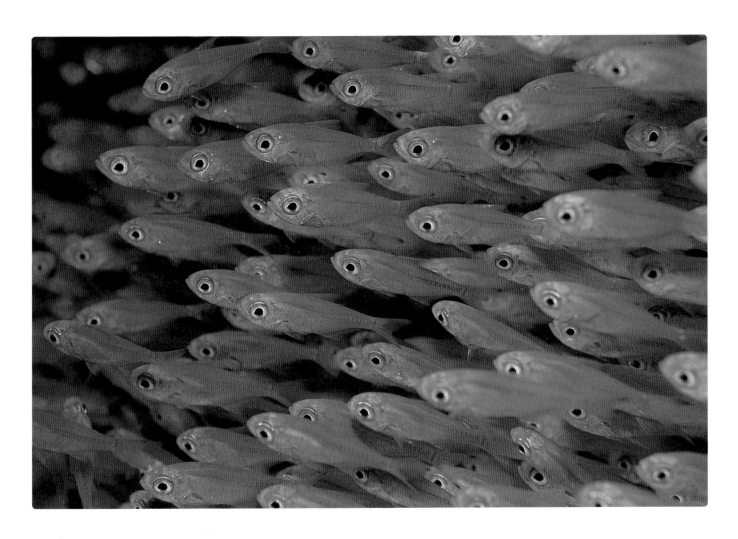

Golden sweeper

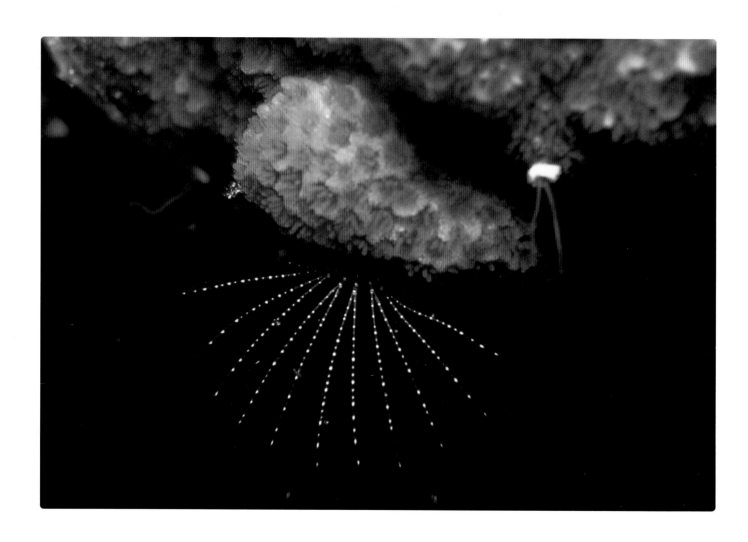

Coral

Christmas tree worm

Trumpetfish

Ocellate pipefish and green algae

Necklace sea star

Burrowing giant clam

Black-spotted dart

Threadfin butterflyfish *(left)* and stars-and-stripes puffer *(right)*

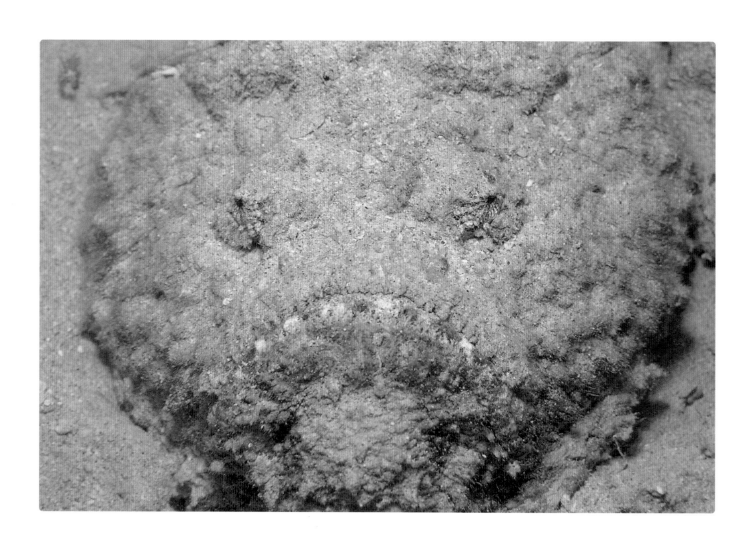

Reef stonefish

Flathead

Nudibranch

Purple-spotted nudibranch

Black feather star and scarlet sea fan

Black-and-yellow feather star

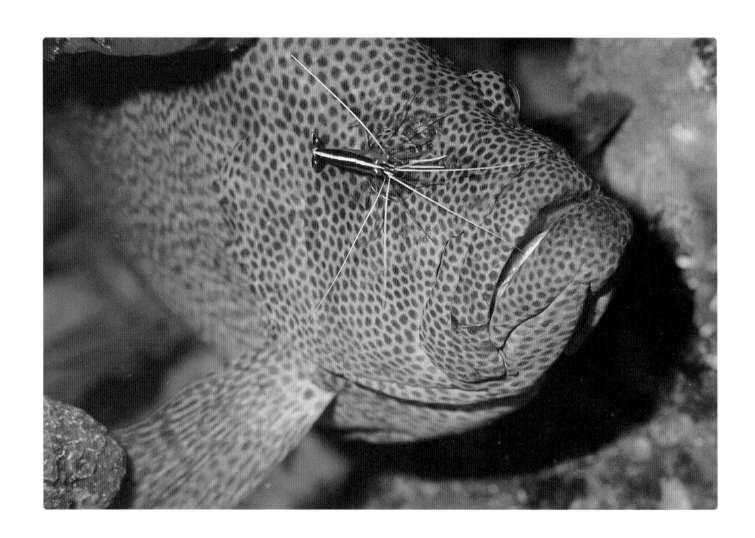

Tomato rockcod and amboin cleaner shrimp

Leopard moray eel and amboin cleaner shrimp

Crocodilefish

Mantis shrimp

Scrawled leatherjacket

Longfin bannerfish

Eggshell shrimp

Imperial shrimp and variegated sea cucumber

Clown triggerfish

Vagabond butterflyfish

Ribbon eel

Lined blenny

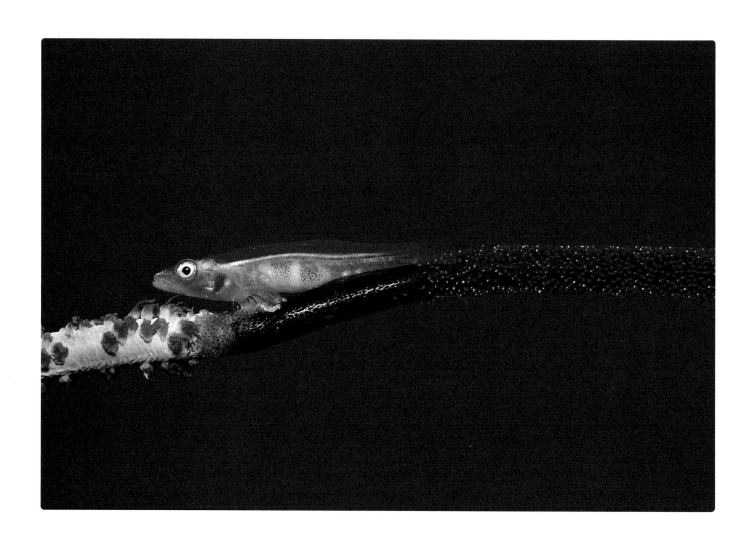

Sea whip goby and sea whip

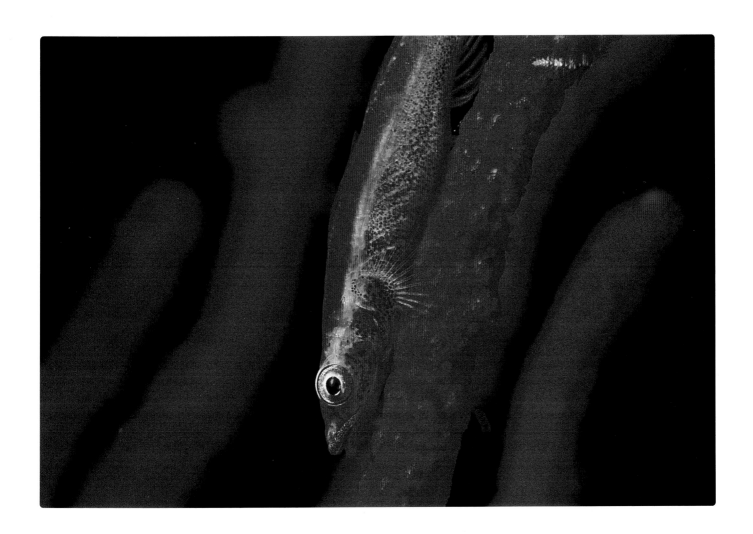

Sea whip goby and red sea fan

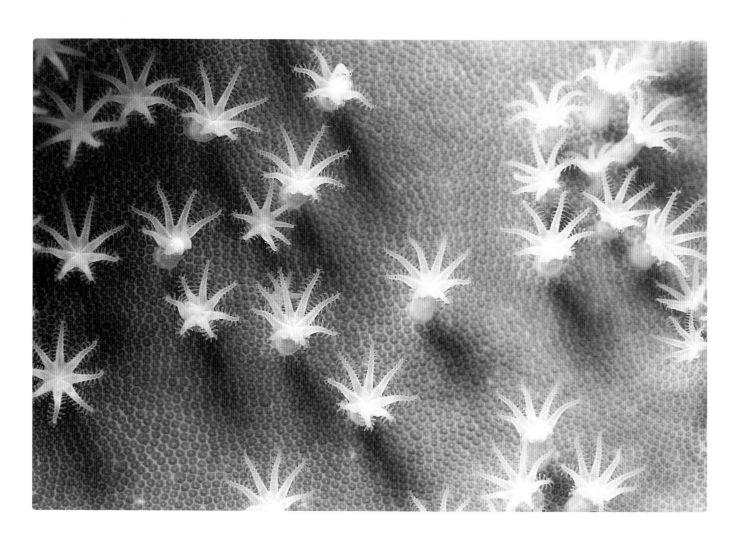

Leather coral

Razorfish

Blue and gold fusilier

Whale shark

Gold-spotted rock skipper and coral

Coral-dwelling hermit crab and reef coral

CAPTIONS

Note: Confirmed identifications of several of the animals could not be made because complete information regarding the location of every shot was not available or because critical information such as the tail color of a fish hiding behind a rock was not available. In those cases an "sp." has been placed after the scientific name to indicate that the species identification could not be made reliably.

PAGE 6. The delicately complex structures built by animals on the reef can be the result of group effort (this colonial pink sea fan) or individual accomplishment (this black radial feather star). **pink sea fan** *Suberqorgia Mollis,* **feather star** *Comanthina schlegeli*

PAGE 9. Whether colonial or individual, reef animals that attach to the bottom (or to other animals) create complex hard skeletons, using minerals dissolved in seawater. The reef-building coral (in the lower left) has secreted a hard structure of calcium carbonate, or limestone. The more flexible branches of the scarlet sea fan are built of a combination of protein and minerals. The black and yellow feather stars, relatives of sea urchins and sea cucumbers, create delicate, but strong and flexible "arms" with thousands of moving parts. **reef coral** *Acropora variabilis,* **scarlet sea fan** *Melithaea ochracea,* **feather star** *Comanthina schlegeli*

PAGE 10. Blue-lined snappers swim on almost every coral reef in the Indo-Pacific and are abundant on Hawaiian reefs. However, before 1950 there were none in Hawaii. Since state fishery biologists introduced them as a game fish, the species has spread rapidly throughout the Hawaiian Islands, perhaps with bad effects on native fishes, who have new competition for food. **blue-lined snapper** *Lutjanus kasmira*

PAGE 11. Individual fish maintain their position in a school both by seeing and by feeling their schoolmates. Fin and body movements cause vibrations that are detected by the lateral line, clearly seen on the sides of these banded jacks. The line begins on the upper side of the body, a short distance behind the eye, curves down to the midline, and extends to the tail. **banded jack** *Uraspis* sp.

PAGE 12. This tiny anemonefish benefits from the protective surroundings of the tentacles of a sea anemone. Along with brothers and sisters, it hatched from an egg in a nest that its parents prepared near the anemone. The expanded ends of the tentacles are far smaller than the diameter of a pea. **juvenile anemonefish** *Amphiprion chrysopterus,* **anemone** *Physobrachia* sp.

PAGE 13. Scientists who study animal behavior have called the bright pigments of reef fishes "poster colors" because they may serve as advertising. Such coloration makes them obvious to other members of the same species, which they may try to attract as mates. The bright patterns of this clownfish also warn off intruders from its anemone home. **clown anemonefish** *Amphiprion ocellaris,* **anemone** *Heteractis* sp.

PAGE 14. The tentacles of sea anemones are covered with tiny, stinging cells like those found in their relatives, the jellyfish. Anemonefish have the ability to develop an immunity to these cells by forming special mucus on their skin surfaces. Such immunity permits them to nestle closely into the protection of the anemone and escape predation by larger fish. **carpet anemone** *Heteractis magnifica* **maldive anemonefish** *Amphiprion nigripes*

PAGE 15. A sea anemone has no skeleton. Its form is changeable and relies on the pressure of the watery fluid contained within its tissues. Thus it can readily change shape, expanding and exposing its tentacles to the water or closing up and protecting them from wave action or curious photographers. **carpet anemone** *Heteractis magnifica*

PAGE 16. The width of this view of a sea anemone is less than an inch. Pigment cells stud the surface of the anemone, providing protective coloration and revealing the location of light-sensitive structures, too simple to really be called eyes. **armed sea anemone** *Dofleina armata*

PAGE 17. Centered in this photograph is the mouth of the anemone, surrounded by tentacles studded with poisonous "thread cells." This view may be likened to a small fish's last sight of the world before it is engulfed by this predaceous relative of corals. The sand in the background reveals this to be a burrowing anemone. **armed sea anemone** *Dofleina armata*

PAGE 18. An irreverent classics scholar might name this scorpion fish "Curly." The elaborate extensions of its skin are called cirri from the Latin word meaning "curls." They camouflage this ambushing predator and help it to look like a plant-covered rock. The large mouth reveals that it is a gulping predator that ambushes its prey, usually a small fish or shrimp, when it unsuspectingly approaches what appears to be a rock. **raggy scorpionfish** *Scorpaenopsis* sp.

PAGE 19. The large, flattened claws of box crabs provide a fortress to protect their delicate mouth parts and stalked eyes. Compare these massive claws with the delicate forelegs of the spider crab on page 88. **box crab** *Calappa* sp.

PAGE 20. Needlefish cruise just below the water surface using their densely toothed, stiff, elongated beaks to prey on small fishes. Their long, strong bodies are favored by tropical fishermen, who catch needlefish at night by blinding them with bright lights. At such times this can be a dangerous fish. Confused, wildly jumping needlefish have been known to leap into a fishing boat, spearing arms and legs, and sometimes inadvertently killing luckless fishermen by fatally jabbing their stiff beaks through their eyes and into their brains. **juvenile needlefish** *Platybelone argalus*

PAGE 21. Although barracuda have a reputation as dangerous solitary predators, most species are schooling varieties harmless to a scuba diver or snorkeler. Barracuda, like many kinds of fish that school near the bright surface of tropical seas, are brilliantly silvered. When lighted from the side, their silver coloration is highly visible and probably useful in helping school members to see one another. But when seen from below by a large predator, the silvery school matches the reflective surface of the water and becomes almost invisible. **chevron barracuda** *Sphyraena qenie*

PAGE 22. Most animals on the reef can be roughly divided into two groups—those that wait for their food to come to them, like this sponge and these wire corals, or those that go out and get their food. The latter includes most mobile animals, such as fish. This rockfish combines both methods by sitting quietly camouflaged by its color and skin flaps. As a prey swims by, it darts out and grabs it. **rockcod** *Sebastiscus marmoratus*, **wire coral** *Cirripathes anguina*, **sponge** *Callyspongia elegans*

PAGE 23. This hermit crab shows two adaptations to its sedentary life-style—expanded featherlike antennae to net small food organisms floating by in the water and expanded claws to form a trapdoor for its tubular home when it retreats from an unwanted visitor. (See page 87 for another view.) **fire coral** *Millepora* sp., **hermit crab** *Paguritta harmsi*

PAGE 24. The scarlet colors and silvery reflections we are accustomed to seeing in underwater photographs present a beautiful but unnatural view of the reef. The opacity of deep water excludes bright light from the depths. This scarlet sea fan would appear black or dark blue without the artificial light of the photographer's strobe. The slender cardinalfish would seem almost invisible because of their delicate, almost transparent bodies. **slender cardinalfish** *Rhabdamia gracilis*, **scarlet sea fan** *Melithaea ochracea*

PAGE 25. This delicate sea anemone seems to be quite exposed on the open sand. But when heavy currents stir up the sandy bottom, the anemone can reduce the water pressure within its expandable tentacles and retract completely into its buried tube. When gentler currents bring floating food, the tentacles expand wave in the current, and catch the meal. **burrowing anemone** *Cerianthus* sp.

PAGE 26. Do fish sleep? Certainly many fish remain immobile during part of a twenty-four-hour cycle. Most day-active fishes seek shelter at dusk and remain motionless during the night. Stationary fishes seem asleep in the daytime. This banded rockcod, however, is on the alert, quietly lying in wait for prey items to swim by. **black-tipped rockcod** *Epinephelus fasciatus*, **octocoral** *Subergorgia suberosa*

PAGE 27. Sex is never simple. It is especially complex and fascinating on the coral reef. This adult male moon wrasse bears the bright colors typical of his gender. He began his life as a differently colored juvenile that matured into a still differently patterned female. After a few years of egg production, her ovaries atrophied, and testes developed. The consequent male sex hormones stimulated this color pattern, and she became he—a distinctively colored male. **male moon wrasse** *Thalassoma lunare*, **feather star** *Comanthina schlegeli*

PAGE 28. These two blennies are engaged in a significant conversation, its content unknown. Because they are different species, it is probably not a friendly chat. Interactions among individual fish on the reef can be attractive, for mating and pair bonding, for example. More frequently they contain aggressive signals such as "Keep away from my food," or "Stay off my turf" or "Go away! Get your own girlfriend." Fishes have many ways of signaling each other, such as the flashing of color pattern and the movement and erection of fins. *(left)* **Yaeyama blenny** *Ecsenias yaeyamaensis, (right)* **neon triplefin** *Helcogramma striata*

PAGE 29. Moving in three-dimensional space (unlike the bottom-sitting blennies on the previous page) these two damselfish pass each other in mid-water. The foreshortening of the picture makes it appear that they are kissing. However, the fish on the left is farther from the camera than the one on the right. The fish on the right is definitely sending a strong statement to the fish on the left, indicated by its erect dorsal fin. **Weber's chromis** *Chromis weberi*

PAGE 30. A spindle cowrie spends its life associated with the red sea fan, feeding on its polyps and depositing eggs on its surface. The red color and white tubercles of this elongated species of marine snail match the sea fan closely and probably afford it protection from predators. **spindle cowrie** *Phenacovolva* sp., **red sea fan** *Mopsella* sp.

PAGE 31. Unlike its relative the spindle cowrie, which spends its life on sea fans, an egg cowrie ranges over the reef. However, it is also a grazing predator, feeding on soft corals. Unlike most of its cowrie relatives, whose shells are variegated and heavily patterned, the egg cowrie has a uniformly white shell. Its black foot and fleshy mantle can be retracted within the shell. **egg cowrie** *Ovula ovum*, **soft coral** (under cowrie) *Sinularia* sp., **hard coral** (upper left and right) *Echinopora* sp.

PAGE 32 The reef is full of danger, usually in the form of a larger animal looking for food. For protection, many shrimp, like this tiny, purple-legged beauty, dwell within the protective tentacles of corals and sea anemones. **anemone shrimp** *Periclimenes* sp., **bubble coral** *Plerogyra sinuosa*

PAGE 33. This tiny triplefin blenny is shorter than half the length of your little finger and far thinner. Its almost transparent body makes it very difficult to detect, and it is even further defended by living amongst a poisonous thicket of fire coral. Well protected from predation, the tiny bigmouth is advantageously situated for preying on small invertebrates as they drift or swim by. **bigmouth triplefin** *Helcogramma* sp., **white fire coral** *Millepora tenella*

PAGE 34. This postage stamp-size patch of skin on the top of a spotted sea slug looks smoother than that on its starfish relative on page 35. But it still reveals the reason for the scientific name for the whole group in which it is classified—Echinodermata, from the Greek for "spiny-skinned." **bronze-spot sea cucumber** *Bohadschia argus*

PAGE 35. This close-up photograph of the underside of a sea star shows an area about as wide as one's index finger. In the center of the red "star" is the single opening that serves as mouth and anus, and through which all food passes, both in and out. To feed, the starfish everts its stomach, covers a patch of live coral, digests it, and withdraws the stomach into its body cavity. Like many marine animals, starfish build their external skeletons by precipitating calcium carbonate (sometimes known as limestone), a compound universally dissolved in seawater. The bright red pigments in this starfish are chemically bonded to the calcium molecules. **pincushion starfish** *Culcita novaguineae*

PAGE 36. Although the coral cod preys on small fish on the coral reef, it harmlessly welcomes the cleaner wrasse to intimate association. The specially adapted teeth and mouth of the cleaner wrasse remove parasites from the mouth and skin of the coral cod. **coral cod** *Cephalopholis miniata*, **cleaner wrasse** *Labriodes dimidiatus*

PAGE 37. Fish are not the only personal groomers on the reef. Several species of shrimp, including this cleaner shrimp, remove parasites and dead skin from the mouths and gills of fishes. **coral cod** *Cephalopholis miniata*, **cleaner shrimp** *Periclimenes* sp.

PAGE 38. Although their relatives, the reef-building corals, construct their rigid skeletons from calcium salts dissolved in seawater, soft corals strengthen their turgid walls with stiff spicules. Such reinforcing bars permit colonies to reach over six feet high when they are fully expanded at night. **soft coral** *Dendronephthya* sp.

PAGE 39. Clownfish are not the only fish to live in close association with members of the great group of animals called Cnidaria—corals, anemones, and jellyfish. The two-lobed goby spends its entire life on the surfaces of soft coral. One must closely inspect a soft coral colony to detect the ubiquitous goby, barely an inch long. **two-lobed goby** *Pleurosicya mossambica*, **soft coral** *Dendronephthya* sp.

PAGE 40. Even tinier than its relative on page 39, this goby is barely longer than the diameter of the polyps of the coral colony on which it lives. **coral** *Tubastraea* sp., **coral goby** *Pleurosicya mossambica*

PAGE 41. When young, scallops are mobile, double-shelled molluscs—relatives of clams, cowries, and nudibranchs. As scallops mature, they attach to the bottom. This red-eyed rock scallop fastens to a coral colony, which eventually grows to surround it. Like other molluscs of tropical reefs, this scallop has well-developed light sensors, seen here surrounded by red pigment. Each light sensor is a primitive eye with light-sensitive nerve cells and a simple lens. **red-eyed rock scallop** *Pedum spondyloideum*, **coral** *Porites* sp.

PAGE 42A. *(left)* With few exceptions, coral reef fishes have two pairs of nostrils, clearly seen between and just in front of the eyes of this black-tipped rockcod. **black-tipped rockcod** *Epinephelus fasciatus*

PAGE 42B. *(right)* Members of the hawkfish family (like this dwarf hawkfish) not only have the sharp eyes of their avian namesake but prey by perching on a coral branch and rapidly swooping down to gulp an unsuspecting fish or shrimp. **dwarf hawkfish** *Cirrhitichthys falco*

PAGE 43A. *(left)* The hard, boxlike body of the cowfish is formed from fused scales. The projections above the eyes—as well as its calm grazing behavior—are responsible for its common name. **thornback cowfish** *Lactoria fornasini*

PAGE 43B. *(right)* Characteristic of members of the hawkfish family, like this golden hawkfish, are the branchlets at the tips of dorsal finrays that help to camouflage the fish by appearing to be algae or coral polyps. **gold hawkfish** *Cirrhitichthys aureus*

PAGE 44. Like the whale shark on page 85, the manta ray is impressively large and makes its living by straining small animals from the water. The fleshy projections, or palps, in front of each eye increase the flow of food-filled water into the mouth. Clinging beneath the manta ray are slender suckerfish. Their suckers—located on top of the head—are a special modification of the muscles and struts of their dorsal fin. **manta ray** *Manta birostris*, **slender suckerfish** *Echeneis naucrates*

PAGE 45. Although jellyfish medusae float freely like some sort of offshore galleon, early in life they are attached to the bottom like their relatives the reef corals and sea anemones. The rough surface of this medusa has given rise to an unflattering common name. **warty jellyfish** *Pelagia* sp.

PAGE 46. The bright color of this purple dottyback reveals it to be male. After its mate deposits a ball of eggs that sticks to the bottom, the male guards the nest of eggs, frequently picking up the ball of eggs with its mouth to shift it around. Although small (as long as an index finger) and delicate, dottybacks are significant predators relative to their size, feeding on small crabs, prawns, and fishes. Look closely at its fins. Each finray is connected by a membrane to the other rays. Several sets of muscles connect each finray to the vertebral column and support complex fin movements used to swim and to communicate with other dottybacks. **purple dottyback** *Pseudochromis porphyreus*

PAGE 47. The threadfin dartfish is well named both for its appearance and its behavior. Dartfish feed by hovering over a rubble bottom, picking small animals from the water column as they swim by. The long trailing tail filaments of this three-inch-long fish occur only in adults. **threadfin dartfish** *Ptereleotris hanae*

PAGE 48. When alarmed by predator or diver, a porcupinefish inflates its body with water to erect its long spines. This relaxed individual shows a clear view of the reason for its scientific name diodon, or "double-toothed." All the upper teeth and all the lower teeth are fused into a beaklike structure used to bite off chunks of coral. (The lower dental ridges are barely visible just behind the white, lower lip.) **freckled porcupinefish** *Diodon holacanthus*

PAGE 49. The ragged-fin firefish is as bright and flickery as a flame. Venom produced at the base of each dorsal spine and delivered on their needle-sharp points can burn the victim with greater pain than any flame. **ragged-fin firefish** *Pterois antennata*

PAGE 50. Each pink tube in this picture contains a retracted white coral polyp. When unthreatened in the daytime, these polyps extend. Each soft-bodied polyp has secreted its own hard calcium tubular apartment. Multiplied by millions upon millions, these tiny polyps build large colonies, the basis for reefs and atolls. **cora** *Acropora valida*

PAGE 51. Many corals and their relatives, like this scarlet sea fan, extend their polyps at night to feed on food that drifts by. **scarlet sea fan** *Melithaea* sp.

PAGE 52. Wide and expansive, coral reefs still provide only a finite amount of living space. Coexistence, the balance among species, is complex. In this picture we see two significant predators—a spotted moray eel and a lionfish—with hundreds of schooling prey. In the upper left corner is the dorsal fin of another lionfish. Although not clearly visible in this photo, there are probably at least a dozen other predators in the space of the reef covered by this photograph. **lionfish** *Pterois volitans*, **moray eel** *Gymnothorax* sp.

PAGE 53. Although schooling behavior affords some protection from being eaten for each individual, only fit and alert school members survive. The lionfish in the center of the picture uses its large and gaudy fins to distract the fish as they swim by. Once they lose their place in the school, the lionfish can quickly engulf them with its large mouth. (Lionfish are close relatives of firefish.) **golden sweeper** *Parapriacanthus ransonneti*, **lionfish** *Pterois volitans*

PAGE 54. This close-up, an inch across, of a mushroom coral reveals the delicate complexity of the coral skeleton constructed by its soft-tissued body. Unlike most reef-building corals, which are colonial, mushroom corals build their skeletons as solitary individuals. **mushroom coral** *Fungia* sp.

PAGE 55. Golden sweepers are nocturnal fish, forming large aggregations in caves during the day and emerging during darkness to disperse and feed on zooplankton. Their relatively large eyes are probably an adaptation for nocturnal feeding and for maintaining dense aggregations in the low light of caves. **golden sweeper** *Parapriacanthus ransonneti*

PAGE 56. Delicacy and durability endure side by side on the coral reef. Behind this pink stony coral projects the feathery filaments of an unidentified filter-feeding animal. **coral** (family *Pocilloporidae*)

PAGE 57. Festively colored Christmas tree worms decorate coral reefs. Sometimes as many as fifty worms can be found in one square yard of reef, creating a colorful grove. These delicate "branches" are actually the feeding arms of worms, straining out food by floating it in the water. When irritated, a worm retracts into its tube, built within a coral colony or rock, and closes a trapdoor to avoid disturbance and damage. **christmas tree worm** *Spirobranchus giganteus*

PAGE 58. With big eyes, strong bodies, and specially adapted mouths, trumpetfish are notable predators on smaller reef fishes. Although the mouth opening looks small, it can engulf fairly large reef fish. The trumpetfish literally sucks them into its mouth. Strong suction is created by reducing the pressure in the mouth as water is forced through the gills with the mouth closed. As the trumpetfish approaches its prey, it quickly opens its mouth, and water is sucked in, bringing a hapless fish with it. Although this trumpetfish is bright yellow, individual animals might be gray, brown, or black. **trumpetfish** *Aulostomus chinensis*

PAGE 59. Resembling a more delicate version of the trumpetfish, the related pipefish feeds in a similar sucking way with its tubelike mouth. Pipefish are actually more closely related to sea horses. In fact, the straight body and similar fin placement of this pipefish resemble a sea horse that has been straightened out. **ocellate pipefish** *Corythoichthys ocellatus*, **green algae** *Chlorodesmis* sp.

PAGE 60. Although the star of this picture is the orange-and-scarlet necklace sea star, the entire surface of the reef shown here is covered by something living—red coralline algae, sponges, and tunicates. This starfish feeds on detritus and fleshy algae. **necklace sea star** *Fromia monilis*

PAGE 61. This close-up of the mantle of a burrowing giant clam shows the importance of sunlight and plant photosynthesis for the clam. Pigmentation forms a kind of sunblock to protect the clam's flesh. Within its tissue are tiny plant cells, zooxanthellae, that—like all plants—use the sun to produce food, some of which nourishes the clam. The tiny dark spots are very simple eyes that help the clam to respond to sunlight. **burrowing giant clam** *Tridacna maxima*

PAGE 62. Although they are very distinct in this photograph, in nature the color pattern of black-spotted darts provides camouflage. The black longitudinal lines on their slender, powerful tails and dorsal and anal fins combine with their silvery bodies to merge into invisibility in the blue waters over the reflective white sand where they prey on smaller fishes. **black-spotted dart** *Trachinotus bailloni*

PAGE 63. Beautiful white sand beaches are famous attributes of tropical islands, but beautiful white sand *bottoms* are directly related to tropical marine life. Home to many kinds of invertebrates like worms, crabs, and shrimp, sandy bottoms provide a feeding ground for fishes like this threadfin butterfly fish.

Almost every grain of sand on the beach or bottom of a coral island was created by a plant or animal and represents fragments of their limestone skeletons. Fishes like the puffer (on the right) use beaklike teeth to chomp off coral branches. They digest the soft coral tissue and defecate the indigestible fragments of coral skeleton, thus adding to the reef's sand supply. Puffers also eat and disintegrate the shells and skeletons of molluscs, sponges, tunicates, crabs, sea urchins, brittle stars, starfish, and hermit crabs. Tropical island beachcombers can examine a handful of white sand and identify the original donors of each fragment—sea urchin spine here, a crab shell there, a coral chunk everywhere. **threadfin butterfly fish** *Chaetodon auriga*, **stars-and-stripes puffer** *Arothon hispidus*

PAGE 64. Look carefully at the center of this picture—stare into the beady eyes of the world's most poisonous fish. Retiring and secretive, stonefish bury themselves in sandy parts of the reef, hiding from unsuspecting prey fish, which they gobble up as they swim by. However, this same secretiveness should cause every wader in tropical Pacific waters (with the exception of Hawaii, where this species is absent) to wear reef shoes and walk with care. A barefoot misstep onto the back of a stonefish brings an injection of deadly venom from its spiny dorsal fin. The consequence is liable to be excruciating pain quickly followed by death. **reef stonefish** *Synancea verrucosa*

PAGE 65. Large mouth, big eyes, and hiding habits are the deadly formula for predator fish like this flathead. An unsuspecting shrimp, crab, or fish swimming over a sandy bottom could find the sand exploding to reveal the gaping mouth of this sandy bottom predator. **flathead** *(family Platycephalidae)*

PAGE 66. Nudibranchs are the shell-less relatives of marine snails. Their flesh often contains toxins and bad-tasting chemicals that provide some protection from being eaten. The distinctive, obvious color patterns advertise this feature to would-be predators. **nudibranch**

PAGE 67. The common name nudibranch is an adaptation of a scientific name that describes the exposed gills of the members of this group. On the left, one can see these special breathing mechanisms. On the right is the head, with its sensory horns. **purple-spotted nudibranch** *Ceratosoma francoisi*

PAGE 68. What appears to be a single delicate scarlet, and, white, and, black featherlike animal is actually two very unrelated organisms. The black arms are those of a feather star, relative to sea stars and sea urchins. The scarlet sea fan is a colony of individual white polyps. **black feather star** *Tropiometra afra*, **scarlet sea fan** *Melithaea ochracea*

PAGE 69. The complex segments and struts of the feather star's arms fan and sweep food-filled water into its central mouth. The bright pigments of feather stars are tightly, chemically bound to the mineral salts that give the animal's skeleton its rigidity. **black-and-yellow feather star** *Comanthus solaster*

PAGE 70. Large fishes like this tomato rockcod (a relative of groupers) permit cleaner shrimp to clean even the surface of their eye of parasites and sloughing tissue. This cleaner shrimp is popular with marine aquarists and in some circles is known as the "GTO shrimp" because the bright red sides and central white stripe are reminiscent of the Italian racing car called "GTO." Less imaginative biologists named it for the Indonesian island where it was first discovered. **Amboin cleaner shrimp** *Lysmata amboinensis*, **tomato rockcod** *Cephalopholis sonnerati*

PAGE 71. Strong, healthy, sharp teeth are vital for the survival of this fish-eating hunter. Regular dental hygiene is provided by cleaner shrimp. **leopard moray eel** *Gymnothorax flavimarginatus*, **Amboin cleaner shrimp** *Lysmata amboinensis*

PAGE 72. Some big-mouthed predators like flatheads (page 65) bury themselves in the sand for camouflage. Others, like this crocodile fish have adaptations like fleshy skin and mottled coloration that make them look like the rocky bottom. Even the eye of this fish is camouflaged, serving the dual function of finding the prey and also hiding from it. **crocodilefish** *Cymbacephalus beauforti*

PAGE 73. Pugnacious and aggressive, mantis shrimps routinely duel with one another for living space and territory. The well-developed stalked eyes provide a good sense of their surroundings and the action of their opponents. The broadened antennal scales can be used as shields and as threatening signals. The mantis shrimp's most powerful weapon for both aggression and hunting rests in its powerful pair of arms which can break the shells of snails or the glass of aquariums. The large, muscular arms are visible below each antennal flap. **mantis shrimp** *Odontodactylus scyllarus*

PAGE 74. What looks like a small, delicate mouth of the scrawled leatherjacket is actually the "business end" of a strong and heavily strutted complex of bones. These support strong teeth that tear off a wide variety of food items from the reef surface, including fire coral, sea whips, sea fans, colonial anemones, and tunicates. **scrawled leatherjacket** *Aluterus scriptus*

PAGE 75. This longfin bannerfish also has a complex mouth, but it is used to individually pluck small food items like shrimp and fish larvae floating in open water. **longfin bannerfish** *Heniochus acuminatus*

PAGE 76. This tiny eggshell shrimp, less than an inch long, lives like its relatives (see pages 32 and 77) in close association with another larger animal that provides a protective home, in this case, a carpet anemone. In this picture we see only a close-up of the anemone's skin. **eggshell shrimp** *Periclimenes brevicarpalis*

PAGE 77. This boldly colored imperial shrimp is always found in association with a sea cucumber. **imperial shrimp** *Periclimenes imperator*, **variegated sea cucumber** *Stichopus variegatus*

PAGE 78A. *(left)* "By their mouths ye shall know them" could be the motto of ichthyologists, the scientists who study fish. Most of the higher classification (and presumed relationships) of fish groups is based on the complex skeletal structure of their mouths. These mouth forms, in turn, are directly related to the food habits of the fish. The clown triggerfish's mouth, brightly rimmed in yellow, reveals the well-used, strong teeth of a fish that makes its living biting off coral branches. **clown triggerfish** *Balistoides conspicillum*

PAGE 78B. *(right)* In contrast, the more delicate mouth of the vagabond butterfly fish plucks coral polyps and algae from the reef surface. **vagabond butterflyfish** *Chaetodon vagabundus*

PAGE 79A. *(left)* The jaws of the blue ribbon eel bear sharp, pointed teeth to pierce its prey. It finds small fish and shrimp partly by smell. The expanded flaps on its nasal tubes help draw scent-filled water into the sensory chambers. The flaps also serve as a device for signaling to other eels. **ribbon eel** *Rhinomuraena quaesita*

PAGE 79B. *(right)* The blenny's large, comb-toothed mouth grazes algae, like the green plants in the lower corner, from the surface of the reef. **lined blenny** *Ecsenius lineatus*

PAGE 80. Sea whip gobies usually make their solitary home on the wiry branch of a sea whip, a relative of corals. These fishes, like their relatives in the goby family, have a pelvic fin in the form of a suction cup on their chest. This specialized fin helps to hold them onto their flexible perch as it waves in the ocean current. **sea whip goby** *Bryaninops yongei*, **sea whip** *Cirrhipathes anguina*

PAGE 81. Occasionally a sea whip goby will colonize a sea fan where its ability to hold onto a flexible branch is still useful. **sea whip goby** *Bryaninops loki*, **red sea fan** *Mopsella* sp.

PAGE 82. This close-up of leather coral polyps (a penny would cover five or six of them) shows the close resemblance of corals to their relatives the sea anemones. The eight tentacles on each polyp also reveal the origin of the scientific name of this special group, the octocorals. The smaller dots are the mouths of siphonozooids (smaller polyps that lack tentacles and specialize in pumping water). Together the polyps form the soft leathery colony. **leather coral** *Sarcophyton* sp.

PAGE 83. These razorfish have strayed from their usual protection in the long spines of the sea urchin. The common posture for these highly adapted fishes is head down, tail up, with their black stripe matching the erect black spines of the urchin. Razorfish pluck small invertebrates from the water with their tubelike mouths. They are called razorfish because their scales are fused into a sharp edge along the belly line. **razorfish** *Aeoliscus strigatus*

PAGE 84. Schooling fusiliers are some of the most obvious fishes along the edge of outer reef drop-offs, silhouetted against the dark blue of deeper water. A scuba diver venturing forth at night will find them absent, because they retire to the reef to sleep. Their colors fade into a nocturnal coloration of white to reddish pink. **blue and gold fusilier** *Caesio teres*

PAGE 85. The largest fish in the sea feeds on animals as small as rice grains, swallowed into a mouth that stretches the full width of its huge head (look carefully at the front of this shark's head; the dark line is the barely opened mouth). This mouth may be huge, but it presents no threat to a human being; divers frequently approach whale sharks and hitch rides on the high dorsal fin, the same triangle that on other sharks is a dreaded sign of danger.

Whale sharks swim near the surface in the waters of all tropical seas. As big as baleen whales (up to thirty-five feet long), like them, they feed by straining small shrimp and fishes from large volumes of water. Special structures on the gills comb out the food, and the strained water is expelled from the gill slits (visible directly in front of the large winglike pectoral fin). **whale shark** *Rhincodon*

PAGE 86. Most blennies are highly active, obvious members of the reef community. They are often called rock skippers because they use both speed and rocky crevices to escape predators. This bug-eyed fellow is a bit more sedentary and colonizes abandoned tube-worm holes in live coral colonies. **gold-spotted rock skipper** *Istiblennius chrysospilus*, **coral** *Leptastrea transversa*

PAGE 87. Hermit crabs typically live in portable homes, such as abandoned shells. This pair of striped-claw hermit crabs choose to live in immobile apartments—deserted tube-worm holes in a coral head. **coral-dwelling hermit crab** *Paguritta harmsi*, **reef coral** *Turbinaria stellulata*

The so-called scientific, or Latin, name of a plant or animal may look technical and irrelevant to the casual reader, but it contains much useful information about the creature to which it is assigned. It is well worthwhile for anyone with an interest in nature to learn a bit about scientific classification. The naming of a new species is not a casual activity; it is highly structured and fraught with responsibility.

All scientists accept two books of rules for the naming of living organisms, *The International Code of Zoological Nomenclature* and the *International Code of Botanical Nomenclature*. These rules are complicated but are essentially based on three principles: (1) every organism shall be named in a consistent way that reflects its relationship with other organisms; (2) no two kinds of animals or plants shall have the same scientific name; (3) in the event that the second principle is accidentally violated, the animal that has had the name longest shall keep its name, and the other shall get a new name.

Because these rules are universally accepted, scientific names are standard all over the world. Common names are easy to understand and are often very descriptive (if you happen to speak the language in which the name is expressed!). However they are not standardized and may vary from one locality to another, or even from one person to another. To an English-speaking scientist or a Serbo-Croatian scientist, the animal on page 44 of this book is *Manta birostris*. By comparison, the common names in their respective tongues are *manta* and *golub uhan*.

A well-considered scientific name can contain a lot of information. On page 20, the name *Platybelone* describes a physical characteristic of the fish: *platy* is Greek for "flat," and *belone* is Greek for "needle." The name describes the flattened needlelike nose of these fish. On page 28, even though a reader may not know where Yaeyama is, the ending -ensis is a tip-off that the first specimen to be named was collected there (resulting in the name *Ecsenius yaeyamensis*). There are also some nuances in naming organisms. Although officially discouraged, "patronymics" are often created to

honor colleagues or collectors. On page 29, *Chromis weberi* honors an important nineteenth century scientist named Weber. Many taxonomists believe that naming a plant or animal after a place or person "wastes" the opportunity to include useful information in the name.

The basic scientific names we usually see for an organism (and the ones that have been provided in this book) comprise two parts, the **genus** and the **species**. The genus (always first and always capitalized, although sometimes abbreviated to its initial letter) represents a group of species that scientists who study them believe to be related to each other. Related genera (plural for *genus*) are classified into families (usually family names end *-idae*). Based on a variety of characteristics, ranging from morphology to biochemistry and fossil history, scientists group families into a hierarchy of classification that represents tentative conclusions about relationships and evolutionary history.

Although there can be subcategories, the major classification divisions are these:

Phylum, Class, Order, Family, *Genus, species*

The only category in this hierarchy that is "natural"—that is not an intellectual construct of the mind of the scientist—is the species.

What is a species? Most people can recognize the members of a species just by looking at them. A mallard duck is a mallard duck, although a naive observer might classify the multi-colored males in a separate group from the brown females. Biologists define a species as an interbreeding population of genetically related organisms whose young (when adult) are essentially similar to the parents, and that retains genetic integrity from generation to generation. Though it is true that some of the members of some species (e.g., tigers, lions, porpoises) will occasionally interbreed with other species in captivity, in nature all species maintain their specific genetic identity and do not interbreed. (Although rare, accidental hybrids may occur in closely related species which broadcast their eggs and sperm, such as reef fish.)

GLOSSARY

Algae (singular is alga) include a variety of marine plants. Some are single-celled (see zooxanthellae); others are complex. None have true stems, leaves, or roots. Coralline algae form calcium carbonate crusts that are important in consolidating coral reefs.

Calcification is the self-impregnation of living plant or animal tissue with calcium salts, especially calcium carbonate, sometimes called "limestone" or "chalk." The hard skeletons of many marine animals (e.g. corals, cowries, clams, sea stars) are the result of calcification.

Classification is the formal, ordered arrangement of living things into hierarchical categories that reflect their presumed relationships. The science of classification is called taxonomy. Nomenclature is the formal system of naming living organisms.

Cleaning behavior is a special transitory relationship of mutual benefit between two animals. A larger animal (usually a fish) permits another, smaller animal (usually a fish or shrimp) to remove, or to clean, parasites and sloughing tissue from it.

Filter-feeding is the process of removing small food items suspended in water currents, usually by straining with a special structure. Animals that filter-feed can be free-swimming (like baleen whales, whale sharks, and anchovies) or attached to the bottom (like barnacles, corals, and feather stars).

Guild refers to a group of animals that, though not necessarily related, feed in a similar way, such as bottom-grazing, plankton-picking, or filter-feeding. The term comes from the Middle English name for craft associations, such as carpenters, glaziers, and ironworkers.

Indo-Pacific refers to the oceanic region (and included coastlines) of intertropical Asia and the western Pacific ocean. Many marine species are widely distributed within the Indo-Pacific region from Hawaii to Sumatra.

Invertebrate is a general name given to any of the millions of kinds of animals that do not have a backbone. Examples include sponges, corals, jellyfish, shrimp, and sea cucumbers. This large group is contrasted with the much smaller group of vertebrate animals, such as fishes, snakes, whales, birds, and humans.

A **larva** is a pre-adult form of an animal that hatches from an egg. It usually looks very different from the adult and leads a distinct life before transformation into the adult form. Most marine larvae drift in the open sea, maturing only when they move into the shallow waters of a reef.

The **mantle** is that part of the body wall of a mollusc (e.g. clam, snail, nudibranch) that secretes the shell and encloses the internal organs.

Ocellate is an adjective that describes the spots in an animal's color pattern. It comes from the Latin word for "little eye."

Photosynthesis is the vital process regularly occurring in green plants that uses the energy of sunlight to manufacture energy-rich compounds (like sugar) from carbon dioxide and water.

Plankton is the great host of plants and animals that drift in the sea's currents. Although some, like fish larvae, have the ability to swim, such movement is effective only on a small scale. All plankton are subject to the movement of ocean currents. "Zooplankton" refers to planktonic animals; "phytoplankton" refers to planktonic plants.

A **polyp** is an individual cnidarian such as coral, anemone, or sea fan which is attached to a surface like a rock, or a colony of related animals. Its body is cylindrical and tentacles usually surround a mouth at the free end.

Reef-building refers to those corals with calcification abilities that are specially enhanced by single-celled algae living within their tissue (see zooxanthellae).

Sex-reversal in reef fishes refers to the change in gender of an individual during its lifetime. Depending on the species, such change can be from male to female or more usually from female to male. Gender reversals are influenced by behavioral and environmental cues and are usually accompanied by distinctive changes in color patterns.

Spicules are small needle- or rod-like structures of silicate or calcium carbonate that support the soft tissues of invertebrates like sponges and soft corals

Symbiosis describes the intimate and often mutually beneficial relationship between two kinds of organisms. Examples include cleaner shrimp and client fish, and zooxanthellae and corals.

A **tentacle** is an elongated, flexible, unsegmented protrusion surrounding the mouth of an invertebrate animal, such as coral polyp or sea anemone. In such animals tentacles usually occur in groups of six, eight, or more.

A **tube foot** is one of a series of tubular appendages in echinoderms (e.g. sea stars, sea cucumbers) linked to one another through a "water-vascular" system and generally used in locomotion.

A **tubercle** is a small rounded prominence, process, or knob, usually formed in marine vertebrates of calcium carbonate.

Tunicates are a group of marine animals that outwardly resemble invertebrates, like sponges and soft corals. However in larval form, tunicates reveal many characteristics shared with the vertebrate, or "chordate," animals. As adults, they are attached to the sea bottom, although there are planktonic forms.

Zooxanthellae are single-celled algae that live within the tissue of various marine animals such as reef-building corals and giant clams. Through photosynthesis, they produce nutrients that benefit their hosts and biochemically enhance the hosts' ability to form calcified skeletons.

BIBLIOGRAPHY

Brown, R. 1956. *Composition of Scientific Words.* Baltimore:Roland W. Brown.

Catala, R. 1986. *Treasures of the Tropic Seas.* New York: Facts on File.

Coleman, N. 1991. *Encyclopedia of Marine Animals.* New York: Angus & Robertson (HarperCollins).

Debelius, H. 1984. *Armoured Knights of the Sea.* Frankfurt am Main: Kernan Verlag.

Faulkner, D. 1974. *This Living Reef.* New York: New York Times Books.

Fielding, A.,1985. *Hawaiian Reefs and Tidepools: A Guide to Hawaii's Shallow-Water Invertebrates.* Honolulu: Oriental Publishing.

Fielding, A. and E. Robinson. 1987. *An Underwater Guide to Hawaii.* Honolulu: University of Hawaii Press.

George, J. D., and J. J. George. 1979. *Marine Life: An Illustrated Encyclopedia of Invertebrates in the Sea.* New York: John Wiley & Sons.

Guille, A., et al. 1986. *Handbook of the Sea Stars, Sea Urchins, and Related Echinoderms of New Caledonia Lagoon* (in French). Paris: Editions de ORSTROM.

Humann, P. 1992. *Reef Creature Identification:Florida, Caribbean, Bahamas.* Orlando, Fl.: Vaughan Press.

Johnson, S. 1982. *Living Seashells.* Honolulu: Oriental Publishing.

Laboute, P., and Y. Magnier. 1979. *UnderwaterGuide to New Caledonia.* Papeete: Les Editions du Pacific.

Mather, P.,, and I. Bennett. 1984. *A Coral Reef Handbook.* Brisbane: Australian Coral Reef Society.

Myers, R. F. 1989. *Micronesian Reef Fishes.*Barrigada, Guam: Coral Graphics.

Newbert, C. 1984. *Within a Rainbowed Sea.* Honolulu: Beyond Words Publishing Co.

Randall, J. E., G. R. Allen, et al. 1990. *Fishes of the Great Barrier Reef and Coral Sea.* Honolulu:University of Hawaii Press.

Robin, B., C. Petron, et al. 1980. *Living Corals:New Caledonia, Tahiti, Réunion, Caribbean.* Papeete: Les Éditions du Pacific.

Steene, R. 1990. *Coral Reefs, Nature's Richest Realm.* Bathurst: Crawford House Press.

Talbot, F., ed. 1984. *Reader's Digest Book of the Great Barrier Reef.*Sydney: Reader's Digest.

Veron, J. E. N. 1987. *Corals of Australia and the Indo-Pacific.* Topsfield, Ma.: Angus & Robertson (Salem House Publishers).

Wilkens, P., and J. Birkholz. 1986. *Invertebrates: Tube, Soft, and Branching Corals.* Wuppertal: Engelbert Pfriem Publishing.

Wood, E. 1983. *Corals of the World.* Neptune, Fla.: TFH Publications.

ACKNOWLEDGMENTS

For assistance in identifying species, my thanks to Dr. Bruce Carlson and Dr. Carol Hopper of Waikiki Aquarium, University of Hawaii; Dr. John E. Randall, Bernice P. Bishop Museum, Honolulu; and Dr. Katherine Muzik of Harvard University; Dr. William Smith-Vaniz, U.S. Fish and Wildlife Service, Gainesville, Florida; Dr. John McCosker and Dr. William Eschmeyer, California Academy of Sciences; and, Helen Kay Larson, Northern Territories Museum, Australia. Additional thanks to Dr. Muzik for reviewing my text. I extend special gratitude to Linda Taylor for manuscript production and extraordinary assistance in all matters.

Although I hope my text reflects my respects for his work, I offer special compliments to Youji Ohkata for the superb images he has brought to us.